WHO IS JESUS?

Gillian Warren

STORIES FROM JOHN'S GOSPEL

A RESOURCE FOR TEACHERS

Scripture Union

130 City Road, London EC1V 2NJ.

ISBN 0 86201 861 7

British Library Cataloguing-in-Publication Data.
A catalogue record for this book is available from the
British Library.

Phototypeset by Intype, London
Printed and bound in Great Britain by Cox and Wyman
Ltd, Reading

*To my grandson Benji whose enjoyment of
these stories encouraged me to complete the
book.*

I am very grateful to my husband, Michael, Ginny
Cox, Harry Cresswell and all those whose
encouragement and help made this book possible.
I am also grateful to my Quest Club who provided
the stimulus for the book.

Contents

Glossary

Council The Council was a group of Jewish leaders under the headship of the High Priest. It decided legal and doctrinal matters concerning the Jewish religion.

Counsellor The name sometimes used by Jesus for the Holy Spirit, whom the Father would send after Jesus' death. He would live in the disciples, remind them of Jesus' teaching, and give them power and courage to tell others about Jesus.

Disciple A learner or follower. The word is often used in the New Testament for Jesus' twelve closest followers, and sometimes refers to a wider group of people, including women, who also followed Jesus.

The twelve close disciples were Simon Peter and his brother Andrew, James and his brother John, Philip, Bartholomew, Matthew, Thomas, James son of Alphaeus, Thaddaeus, Simon the Patriot and Judas Iscariot.

High Priest The supreme head of the Jewish religion, he led the Council of the Jews, which decided all legal and doctrinal matters concerning the Jewish religion.

Hosanna The word means 'Save now!'. It was used by the crowds when Jesus entered Jerusalem riding a donkey. The Jews were looking for a Messiah-king who would free them from Roman rule and set up an everlasting kingdom.

Jordan River This river flows from Mount Hermon in the far north, through the Sea of Galilee and the Jordan valley to the Dead Sea. It flows through the deepest rift valley on earth, the Dead Sea being almost thirteen hundred feet below sea level.

Messiah Hebrew title meaning 'anointed one'. The nation of Israel had looked forward to the coming of a Messiah-king who would establish his universal and everlasting kingdom. This hope was very much alive during the time of Jesus, and many identified Jesus as the long-awaited Messiah.

Moses The leader sent by God to bring his people out of Egypt into the Promised Land of Israel. During their travels, the people went to Mount Sinai in the desert, and there God gave Moses the Commandments, which are still the basic laws of Jews today.

Passover A very important annual Jewish festival celebrating the deliverance of God's people from Egypt around 1280 BC.

Pharisees A strict religious sect who kept very rigidly to the Jewish law, often adding extra rules and regulations which were very hard and burdensome to keep.

Pontius Pilate The Roman Governor appointed by Caesar. He governed Judaea from 26–37 AD He lived in Jerusalem in a fortified palace called the Praetorium.

Prophet One who speaks in God's name and with his authority. Famous Old Testament prophets include Elijah, Isaiah, Jeremiah and Daniel.

Sabbath The Jewish day of rest, instituted by God

in the fourth commandment. The Pharisees added many rules about the Sabbath which were not in the original law.

Son of God   A title used of Jesus. It signifies the eternal relationship between the Son and the Father, and the absolute Godhead of Jesus.

Synagogues   Local places of Jewish worship. These were first set up when the Jews were in exile, where there was no temple. Only the men took an active part in services; the women and children listened from a screened gallery.

The Temple   The centre of Jewish worship. The Temple of Jesus' day was built by King Herod. It was a magnificent structure, enclosing an area of 35 acres and standing 100–150 feet above ground level at its southern end. It was covered in so much gold that it was a dazzling sight in the bright sun. Part of the walls and the platform where sacrifices were made are still in existence today, although the building was destroyed by the Romans in AD 70.

The wedding of the year

The wedding took place in Cana, a village in the hills of Galilee. It was a cause of great excitement for the whole community. Feasting on these occasions often went on for several days.

The bridegroom and bride were dressed as elaborately as they could afford, with jewels and embroidered clothes. The bridegroom would go in procession to the bride's home, and would bring her back to his home for the wedding feast.

Darkness falls early in Israel, so the roadway would be lit by oil lamps carried by the guests.

The stone jars each held up to one hundred gallons of water, for the use of guests to wash before the feast.

To run out of wine was a terrible social disgrace. Jesus saved the hosts from this embarrassment by his action.

'Mother! Mother! Have you washed my robe for tonight?'

'Hey, Dad! Are the torches ready? Shall I trim the wicks of the lamps?'

'Yes, and fill them with oil too, son, but don't spill it, will you?'

Families all over the village were getting ready for the celebrations. In the bridegroom's home, the servants were hard at work preparing the feast. And boy! it was going to be some feast!

'Fetch more water from the well, Samuel, will you?'

'Get the tables set up.'

'Check the wine, Daniel, please. Must be just right, and plenty of it.'

The servants rushed to and fro as the steward gave orders.

After a hectic day, the heat of the sun gave way at last to a pleasant, early evening breeze.

'Light all the lamps,' ordered the house steward. 'Bring all the food to the table. Then go and tidy yourselves. The guests will be here in an hour.'

The servants hurried to do as they were told. Then one stopped and pointed.

'Look! Here comes the bridegroom!' he told the others as the bridegroom, his parents and his brothers all appeared, dressed in their best clothes. 'The young master looks very smart, doesn't he?'

'His companions are handsome too!' grinned a servant girl.

At the bride's house, there was great joy and excitement as the bride came out in her beautiful wedding gown. It was of white linen, the bodice embroidered with gold and silver thread. She wore a silver necklace, a present from the bridegroom, and over her face a fine veil.

'Wow!' whispered a servant.

'Never seen her look so lovely,' sighed another.

'See the head-dress with those shining bells!' exclaimed a third.

'And the coins on her forehead! Look how they glint in the torchlight!'

'Make way for the bride's attendants,' called the bride's father with a chuckle, and four smiling girls came forward to take their place with the bride. Their long dresses were of soft blue, with coloured embroidery on the bodice, and they all wore jewelled necklaces.

Now everyone was ready and the sense of excitement mounted as they eagerly awaited the arrival of the bridegroom's procession.

'Listen! I hear music!' exclaimed one of the attendants.

The sound of tambourines, cymbals and pipes grew louder every moment. Everyone surged to the doorway and jostled each other to see down the street.

What a wonderful sight it was! The street was lined with flaming torches. There were flickering lamps moving like fireflies as the people crowded around the bridegroom. The bridegroom himself was leading the procession, splendid in his purple wedding robe, with his best man and close friends beside him, and his family all around.

Soon the procession arrived, and the bridegroom walked forward to claim his bride. The crowd grew quiet as he took her two hands in his, and kissed her on the cheek.

'You are beautiful, my love,' he whispered. She smiled at him radiantly.

Then he led her from her home, and together they set off down the street, amid cheering and clapping, music and laughter and singing. Girls were dancing for joy, and the children ran around, shouting with delight.

'Come on,' called eight-year-old Reuben, the bride's youngest brother. 'Let's get to the front!'

He grabbed his older sister by the hand, and they ran off together, pushing their way through the grown-ups to get to the front of the crowd.

'It looks as if the whole of Cana's here!' said his sister, Joanna.

'Of course,' Reuben grinned. 'No one wants to miss the fun!'

They joined in the dancing and cheering, as the happy procession wound its way along the narrow street to the bridegroom's home.

Then the guests went in and settled themselves at the long tables for the feast.

'Wow!' exclaimed Reuben. 'I've never seen so much food,' and his eyes gleamed with joy.

'Now don't be greedy, or you'll be sick,' warned Joanna.

Everyone was laughing and talking, as the servants went round filling their goblets with wine and replacing empty dishes with full ones.

'Isn't that Aunt Mary from Nazareth?' Joanna said, looking down the table.

'Yes, I think so,' said Reuben.

'And that's her son, isn't it, the one who's the carpenter?'

'Who are all the others with him?'

'I don't know. Must be friends of his. They don't come from Cana – or Nazareth, as far as I know. Never seen them before.'

Far into the night the party continued. The guests relaxed and ate and drank their fill.

Suddenly, Mary noticed a very anxious look being exchanged between two of the servants. One whispered something. The other looked horrified and shook his head in disbelief. Quietly, Mary slipped from the table and went across to them.

'Is something wrong?' she asked.

'We've run out of wine.'

'What! Completely?'

'Yes, completely. We've searched everywhere.

There's no more anywhere.'

'You're absolutely sure?'

'Absolutely.' Then he wailed, 'Oh, what are we to do? I can't believe it! How can it have happened? We had so much. More than we thought we could possibly need.' He was near to despair.

'Hold on a moment,' Mary touched his arm, and then cast her eyes around the room, as if looking for someone. She spotted her son in earnest conversation on the far side of the table, and made her way to him. Bending low so that no one else would hear her, she whispered into his ear, 'Jesus, they've run out of wine.'

He looked up into her anxious face. He glanced across at the servants, whispering together. At once, he understood the situation, but he looked at his mother again.

'This isn't really your concern,' he said gently. 'And my time hasn't come yet.'

Mary returned to the servants.

'Just do exactly what he tells you,' she advised them. Then she went back to her place at the table.

Jesus got up slowly, and went to the servants. He beckoned them outside, and pointed to the huge clay jars which had held water for the guests to wash in.

'Fill those with water,' he told them.

The servants looked puzzled, but they grabbed every carrying jar they could find, and some torches, and set off for the well in the dark.

'What good'll that do?' muttered one. 'It's wine we need, not water.'

'How do I know?' replied another crossly. 'Seems daft to me.'

'I watched his face,' said Daniel. 'He's got some kind of plan, I bet.'

'Yes. He looked as if he knew what he was doing.'

'Bah! Fancy coming all this way in the middle of the night to fetch *water*! It's daft, I tell you. Who wants to wash now anyway?'

They were back before too long, and emptied their jars into the large ones till they were brimming full. Then they looked at Jesus questioningly.

'Now draw some out and take it to the chief steward,' he said.

The servants looked at each other, shrugged, and did as they were told. Nervously, one of them filled the chief steward's goblet, took it to him and stood back, waiting. He half-expected to be in serious trouble for daring to serve water.

The steward drank a mouthful. He sniffed the liquid and drank again, and a smile crossed his face. He called down the table to the bridegroom, 'Here, this wine is superb! Most people serve the best first, and offer ordinary stuff when everyone's had plenty. But you've kept the best till now!'

The bridegroom looked pleased, and a little puzzled, but said nothing. The servants looked at one another in relief and astonishment. They hurried to fill every goblet, then gathered outside the door.

'He did it!'

'He changed it!'

'It really *is* wine now, and the best too!'

'But it was water a minute ago. How come . . .?'

'Come off it, Joses! We don't know! He did it! That's what! And we know it! What more do you want?'

'That's the most fantastic thing I've ever seen!'

'Who is he, anyway? Isn't he the carpenter from Nazareth, Joseph's son, Jesus?'

'Yes, but he must be a whole lot more than that to do this!'

'But look at him. He looks like all the rest.'

'He does now, but when he spoke to us earlier, he seemed to know exactly what to do. I mean, I wouldn't have wanted to disobey him, would you?'

'No way! I'm sure he's someone special ... but who?'

Excitement at Sychar

Sychar is in Samaria, the region between Judaea and Galilee. The Samaritan people were despised and hated by the Jews as being of mixed race and religion. Jesus often travelled through Samaria on his way between Galilee and Jerusalem. On this occasion, he astonished his disciples by engaging a woman in conversation (women were considered very inferior in that society). He went further, by accepting hospitality from the Samaritan people. No Jew would even cross the threshold of a Samaritan house, let alone eat or sleep there.

The Messiah, or 'Anointed One', was the longed for king and prophet whom the Jews expected God to send.

The well where Jesus sat down to rest, known as 'Jacob's Well', is situated in the modern town of Nablus on the West Bank in Israel.

It was hot. The sun burned down from a cloudless blue sky and hardly a breeze stirred, even in the hills of Samaria. When it did, clouds of dust whirled up the street, getting into the children's eyes, settling over everything.

It was midday. The time when no one went out, staying in the shade till the sun lost some of its cruel heat. A woman opened her door. She wore a tatty, red dress, and a shawl pulled well over her head and face. She looked up and down the street. No one there. Good. She picked up her water jar and set off to the well.

Tabitha preferred not to be seen. She was known to everyone as 'the bad woman', and people turned away or crossed the street to avoid her, pulling their children close as if they might be dirtied if they got too near.

'All my life I've looked for love, and I've never found it,' she sighed. 'I've just been used and thrown away like an old rag. And now, even this man treats me like a slave. But I've nowhere else to go . . .' A lump came to her throat and hurt. 'No money, no friends, nothing . . .'

She picked her way barefoot along the dusty, stony path, and approached the well, which was surrounded by a low stone wall. Then she gasped – for a man was sitting on the low wall. He looked hot and tired. She hesitated, not wanting to meet him, but it was too late. He was already speaking to her.

'May I have a drink please?' Jesus asked, and she could see that he was badly in need of one. But she also saw that he was a Jew, and Jews never even spoke to Samaritans. They despised them.

'You are a Jew, and I'm a Samaritan,' she said in astonishment. 'Are you really asking *me* for a drink?'

'If you only knew God's good gifts, and who I am, you would be asking me for life-giving water.'

'But sir, you haven't got a bucket, and it's a deep well. How would you get that water? And anyway, what do you mean by "life-giving water"?' She frowned, because she couldn't see what Jesus was talking about.

'Anyone who drinks water from this well will soon be thirsty again,' he explained. 'But whoever drinks the water that I give him will never thirst again. The water I'm talking about will become like a spring inside him, bubbling up all the time and giving him a new life that lasts for ever.'

'Oh please sir, give me that water! Then I'll never be thirsty, and never have to come to the well for more!'

'Go and get your husband and come back.'

'I haven't got a husband.' She blushed with shame and embarrassment.

'No, you're right. You've been married five times, and you're not married to the man you're living with now.'

The woman backed away, very shaken to think that Jesus knew so much about her.

'You must be a prophet, sir,' she said, feeling very uncomfortable.

She tried to change the conversation and started to talk about religion. Then a thought came to her very strongly and she blurted out, 'I know that the Messiah is coming one day. He'll tell us everything.' And she looked at him carefully. He returned her gaze with steady, gentle eyes.

'I am he,' Jesus said quietly.

The woman started backwards, her jaw dropped, and she stared at Jesus, wide-eyed.

'Hurry up, Andrew! We're all hungry and you've got the bread.'

'I'm doing my best,' came a panting voice, 'but it's so hot, and I'm parched with thirst.'

'So am I,' muttered Philip, trying to balance some fruit and cheese in his hands.

The woman turned to see a group of young men coming to the well, each clutching food of some kind, and chatting cheerfully as they came.

They saw her too, and stopped dead in their

tracks. Jesus, talking with a woman! Whatever
would he do next? They looked at one another and
shrugged, but no one said anything.

The woman saw her chance. She put the jar down
and ran back to the town, all thought of the heat,
and of her own shame, forgotten.

'Come quickly!' she called to everyone she found.
'There's a man at the well who's just told me everything I've ever done. Could he be the Messiah? Oh
do hurry! He may be gone soon. He asked me for
a drink... and we got talking ... Please come
now ...'

And they did. Quite a crowd of men, women and
children followed her to the well, where Jesus'
friends sat about under the trees, and Jesus was
seated on the wall of the well.

'That's the one,' the woman pointed excitedly. 'Go
closer. What do you think?'

Jesus looked up and welcomed them all with a
smile.

'Come and share our food,' he invited them. But
they weren't hungry. They just stared silently at
him and his friends. Then one spoke up, 'You've
come a long way and it's hot. Why not stay with us
in Sychar for a day or two, all of you? We'd be glad
to put you up ...'

Then he suddenly realised he was talking to Jews,
who wouldn't dream of even going into a Samaritan's home, let alone eating with him.

Jesus grinned at his friends and said, 'We'd love
to stay, wouldn't we?'

So they all got up and followed the people of
Sychar into the town.

The next two days were amazing for the people of
Sychar. Jesus spoke to them for hours. He talked

about God as if he knew him. He told them that God loved them, that he longed for them all to know and love him, and to be friends with one another. He healed sick people, comforted sad ones, played with the children and told them wonderful stories. He ate meals with anyone who invited him ... and as the people of Sychar listened and watched him, more and more of them began to believe that he was someone special.

'He must be from God,' they said to one another. 'He's so completely different from every other teacher we've heard.'

'He really loves us!'

'He healed my little Sarah!'

'He doesn't mind who he talks to. He treats us all the same!'

'Nothing ever upsets him either, and his eyes, they're so kind.'

'Yet they twinkle when he laughs, and they're almost on fire when he's teaching sometimes. Haven't you noticed?'

The woman who'd met him first was there too. They were beginning to accept her now.

'He's given me a new life,' she said simply. 'The day I met him, I was ready to die. There didn't seem any point in living any more. And then ... he changed it all. Gave me hope. Made me feel ... well, clean, I suppose. I'm sure he's from God.'

Many agreed with her, though some looked doubtful.

'We didn't know what to think when you first called us to meet him, but now we've heard him for ourselves. We've seen the kind of things he does, and we're really sure. He must be the Messiah, the one we've been waiting for.'

Life or death for Capernaum boy

Capernaum was a fishing town by the Sea of Galilee. Cana lay in the hills, some twenty miles to the west. The boy's father was a member of King Herod's court, a man of high social standing.

A rabbi was responsible for the teaching of the boys in each village. Girls stayed at home and learned domestic skills from their mother. The rabbi taught in the local synagogue.

'Mother, Mother!' called a very weak, trembling voice. 'A drink, Mother, please . . .' and the boy's head rolled sideways on the pillow.

His whole body was on fire with fever. He groaned in pain, and his breath came in short, quick gasps.

His mother came running, a cup of water in her hand.

'Here you are. Let me hold your head while you drink.'

But Simon was too weak. His mother put drops of water on his tongue with her own finger. She damped a cloth and tried to squeeze the moisture between his lips. He could barely swallow, yet he longed for a drink. His eyes filled with tears at his own weakness.

'Don't worry, Simon. We'll get you well.' His mother tried to comfort him, as she bathed his forehead and hands with the cool, damp cloth, but she felt desperately worried. What could they do? Was there help anywhere? She couldn't think of any. She was too worried to think clearly. She ran from the room to find her husband, who was an important official at King Herod's court.

'Amos, he's so ill this morning,' she wept. 'I don't think he can last much longer . . .'

'Shhh, it can't be that bad.'

'Yes, yes, it is, I'm sure. I've seen fever before, but not like this. He can't even lift his head to drink, and he hasn't the strength to swallow. Oh, what are we going to do?'

A servant appeared in the doorway.

'Excuse me, sir . . .'

'What is it, Joses?'

'Well, sir, do you remember the teacher from Nazareth, sir, who was here a while ago? I've heard he's recently returned from Jerusalem and is up in Cana at the moment. I was wondering whether . . .'

'Oh yes!' cried Simon's mother. 'If anyone can help, he can.'

'But Cana's twenty miles away. By the time I get there and bring him back, it will be late evening. Will Simon last that long?'

'I don't know. Who can tell? But anything's worth a try.'

Suddenly Simon's father made up his mind.

'Very well, I shall go. Joses, send word to the Governor that I have to be away on urgent business for two days. Get two horses saddled immediately. You and I shall ride to Capernaum at once.'

'I'll pack up some food for your journey,' offered his wife. 'It'll be yesterday's bread, I'm afraid . . .'

'Not to worry. Just something to keep us going, and a skin of water. It'll be a hot ride.'

There was an air of excitement in Cana that morning. Everyone was up early, for the teacher was here.

'What d'you think he'll do this time?' chuckled Samuel, who remembered the night of the wedding. 'More wine? Perhaps a load of extra bread or cheese?'

Daniel sighed. 'He's not a conjuror, you know. He only made the wine 'cos he was sorry for them.' He thought for a moment. 'Of course, if he feels sorry for someone, he *might* do something. Ever so kind, he is.'

'The mistress says we can go and listen to him today. She says we can leave the work till later. Are you coming?'

'Yes, I'm coming,' replied Daniel. 'Give me time.' He stood up slowly, and pulled his cloak around him.

Further down the street the rabbi was muttering crossly.

'Where are my boys this morning? They've never been as late as this. How can I teach them if they don't come at the proper time?'

'They've gone to hear the teacher, rabbi. Aren't you coming too?'

'Certainly not! All this excitement about a young man from Nazareth! *Nazareth*, I ask you! Whoever heard of a teacher, or anybody of any interest or importance, coming out of Nazareth? Where are my boys? Send them here if you see them!' And he stumped away down the street in the opposite direction to everyone else.

On the hillside at the edge of the village, a group had already gathered. Jesus was there, with a number of friends, chatting and laughing. An ever-growing crowd of fathers and mothers, masters and servants, young people and children, was settling on the ground or on low rocks, waiting for Jesus to begin.

The people had been there for hours, and the sun was high and hot in the sky, when a few heads turned at the sound of horses' hooves. Into view came an official and his servant, their horses running with sweat. Their own faces were soaked too, their robes clinging damply to their bodies.

By now, more and more people were turning to see what was going on, and Jesus stopped talking. Clearly, these men were on urgent business.

Amos dismounted hastily, gave the reins to his servant and went immediately to Jesus.

'Sir,' he panted, falling at Jesus' feet. 'My son's dying. Please would you come at once to Capernaum and heal him?' He held out his hands pleadingly. 'Please, sir, please . . .'

For a moment, Jesus appeared not to hear him. He was looking at the crowd.

'None of you will ever believe unless you see me do miracles,' he said sadly.

'Oh sir!' cried the official, not understanding what Jesus was saying. 'If you don't come soon, my son will die.'

Jesus looked at Amos. 'Go home,' he said. 'Your son is going to live.'

The father hesitated, looking intently at Jesus. Then somehow he knew that the words he'd heard were true, 'Your son is going to live.' He got up, looking very gratefully at Jesus. Slowly he turned, walked back to his servant, and said, 'Get the horses dried off and fed and watered. We'll find shelter here for tonight, and set off at dawn tomorrow.'

'But the teacher . . . isn't he coming too, sir?'

'Er . . . no, he's not coming.'

'But, sir, what about Simon?'

'Joses, it's going to be all right. Jesus said, "Your son is going to live," and I believe him.'

'But, sir . . .'

'No more questions, Joses. See to the horses.'

'Yes, sir. Very good, sir.' Joses picked up the two sets of reins and led the horses towards the village.

Next morning, as soon as there was enough light to ride safely, Amos and Joses set off for Capernaum. The journey was downhill much of the way, with the sun behind them, so they made better speed than the day before. By mid-morning they saw the Sea of Galilee glinting in the sun. They rode on, eager to get home and learn the news.

Joses had sharp eyes.

'Sir, isn't that people waving down there, just by the olive grove?'

Amos shaded his eyes with his hand and squinted into the bright sun.

'Something is moving, but I can't see what.'

They trotted nearer.

'Yes, it's two of the house servants, sir. I recognise them. They're waving, and they look excited.'

'Come on, Joses,' urged the official, as he kicked his tired horse to a canter.

Soon they were within hearing distance, and within seconds, they were reining in the horses.

'Simon's all right, sir! The fever's gone! He's had food and drink, and he's able to sit up.'

Amos was filled with happiness, relief and joy.

'When did he start to get better?' he asked.

'Yesterday, at about one in the afternoon, he turned over, opened his eyes, and smiled at his mother. She gave him a drink and he took it without any problem. He asked for food too . . . and soon he was sitting up.'

Amos thought back to the previous day. One in the afternoon. The very hour when he must have been speaking to Jesus!

'Then it's true! Jesus has healed him!'

The official explained to his servants what had happened. 'We found Jesus, and I begged him to come home with us, but he just looked at me and said, "Go home. Your son is going to live." There was something about the way he said it. I . . . I couldn't help believing him. And he's done it!'

He turned to Joses. 'Come on, let's get home! I want to see Simon!' They cantered off in a cloud of dust.

Healing at the Pool

The pool of Bethesda was near the Temple in Jerusalem. Its spring water was believed to have healing properties, and porticos had been built there to give shade to the sick, who hoped for healing. They believed that an angel periodically disturbed the water, and the first person to step into the pool after this would be healed. The man in the story was much too disabled ever to reach the water first. This explains his bitter reply to Jesus.

The Pharisees were angry with Jesus for healing on the Sabbath, as they considered this to be work, and therefore against the law.

Jesus' twelve closest friends are referred to as his disciples. The word 'disciple' literally means 'learner' or 'follower'. These men spent three years with Jesus, the entire time of his public ministry.

It was a warm spring day as a group of young men came down the Mount of Olives, over the Kidron Stream, and up towards the Temple in Jerusalem. They were tired. They'd walked all the way from Galilee, with little chance to rest. But they were happy too, and chatted as they walked along. It was exciting being with Jesus. You never knew what was going to happen next.

Today, Jesus turned right, not going through the

Beautiful Gate into the city, but round towards the Sheep Gate. His disciples followed him, curious. Why this way? They'd never come through the Sheep Gate before.

As they approached the Bethesda pool of water, bordered by fine arches, John turned to Philip. 'Just look at all those sick people under the arches!'

'Looks as if some of them are blind, and some can't walk,' Philip answered.

'They look as if they've been there for years,' John said sadly. 'Do you think Jesus . . .?'

'I doubt it,' answered Thomas, overhearing the conversation. 'There's too many of them, and they've been ill so long.'

'*That* wouldn't bother him,' chipped in Peter. 'He can do anything!'

'We'll soon see,' grinned Andrew.

Jesus made his way towards the arches, his eyes resting on one particularly sick man. He couldn't even sit up, but lay in a bent position on an old, grubby mat. His hair was tangled, and his face was screwed up with pain and bitterness.

Jesus spoke to him, 'Do you want to be well?' he asked.

The man looked up from his mat. What a strange question! Why had he been hanging around this rotten pool all these thirty-eight years if he didn't want to be well? And who was this man anyway? It was none of his business.

'Can't you see?' he exclaimed crossly. 'I can't move by myself, and there's no one around here who's willing to help me get to the pool when the water stirs. While I'm struggling down, someone always gets there first. I haven't a hope.'

The sick people waited by the pool for the water to stir, because they believed that the first person in the pool after it stirred would be healed.

Jesus looked into those sad and angry eyes. 'Get up!' he told him. 'Pick up your mat and walk!'

The man began to feel strength coming into his arms, his back, his legs, his feet. He found he could move his ankles. His neck seemed to hold his head up . . . and before he had time to think any further, he was getting up. He swayed unsteadily as he stood up. Then he bent carefully and rolled up his filthy old mat, tucking it under his arm.

He looked at Jesus. He looked at Jesus' friends who were staring at him in amazement. He turned to look at all the sick people he'd come to know so well and grumbled at so often for years and years. He staggered a little, and then tried to walk. One foot, the other foot . . . it worked! He could walk! He was well!

'Look at me!' he cried out excitedly. 'I can walk! I'm healed!'

The people stared at him. Some of the sick people were jealous. 'Why should he get healed, and not us?' they wanted to know. 'What's so special about him?'

'His bad temper, maybe!' joked a blind man crouching by one of the archways. And everyone laughed bitterly.

The healed man made his way towards the Temple, and was soon surrounded by Jewish officials. They picked on him at once.

'Here, it's the Sabbath today! Put that mat down! It's against the law to carry a mat on the Sabbath!'

'But the man who healed me said to me, "Pick up your mat and walk." '

'Who is he, then? How dare he tell you to do such a thing! What's his name? Where is he?' The officials became more and more angry.

'I-I don't know. I-I couldn't tell you,' the man answered nervously. 'He'll be among this crowd somewhere, I expect, but it'll be hard to find him. There are so many people ...'

Later on, Jesus met him in the Temple.

'Look, you're well now,' he said to him. 'Make sure you don't do wrong any more. No more anger or bitterness. Otherwise something even worse might happen to you.'

The man who'd been healed felt ashamed. He realised that Jesus knew what a horrible, bad-tempered person he'd been. He wanted to say sorry, but instead he went to tell the leaders that it was Jesus who had healed him.

The leaders were furious. 'Jesus, was it? He's a menace, that man. Breaking the Sabbath laws and causing a public disturbance.'

'And it's not the first time either. There's always trouble when he's in the city.'

'Who does he think he is, carrying on as if he could make his own rules?'

'Come on, let's go and deal with him once and for all.'

When they found Jesus, they gathered round him. 'Who do you think you are, healing a man on the Sabbath? And telling him to carry his mat too? Don't you know the law?'

'You're a trouble-maker, you are! The sooner we get rid of you the better.'

Jesus spoke quietly. 'My Father is always doing things, and I must do them too,' he said.

The Jewish leaders knew that Jesus was speaking about God as his Father, and this made them angrier than ever.

'How dare you call God your "Father" like that!

You're claiming to be equal with God!'

'Dangerous lies!' shouted another. 'He should be silenced immediately!'

From then on, the Jewish leaders began to plot against Jesus, although more and more people followed him.

Food for thousands

The action takes place round the northern shore of the Sea of Galilee, a large lake approximately twelve by eight miles in size. Apart from a few houses near the shore, belonging to local fishermen, the hillside was open and uninhabited. The idea of buying food for so many people was absurd! The story is presented as a dramatic reading.

Scene 1 The beach at Capernaum.

Narrator: There was great excitement down by the lake. Jesus had been healing lots of people. More and more were crowding in to look and gape in astonishment.

Jesus: (*to his disciples*) Come on! You've been hard at work and you could do with a rest, and so could I. Let's go off somewhere quiet for a while.

Narrator: Peter looked at Jesus questioningly and pointed to his boat. Jesus nodded.

Peter: Andrew, give us a hand, will you?

Narrator: Together, they shoved the heavy wooden boat down the beach into the water.

Peter: (*to the others*) In you get!

Narrator: One by one they splashed through the water and climbed into the boat.

Thomas: (*anxiously*) Where are we going?

Matthew: (*yawning*) Somewhere peaceful, that's all that matters. I could sleep for a week. This preaching and healing's all very well, but it's far more tiring than tax collecting ever was!

Peter: (*to Jesus*) Where to, Master?

Jesus: Head north-east. We should be able to land and find a quiet place over there in the hills.

Narrator: Jesus' friends started rowing the boat out to sea. The breeze was blowing in their faces. The water lapped against the side of the boat. They were happy to be away from the crowd, and alone with Jesus.

Meanwhile, two boys made a plan as they watched the boat setting out to sea.

Mark: Joel, quick, let's run round the end of the lake. We might get there before they do!

Joel: Who?

Mark: Jesus and his friends, stupid! They've just gone off in a boat, but there's quite a headwind. I reckon we could beat them.

Joel: What d'you want to do that for? I was going to help Dad with the nets this afternoon.

Mark: Your dad's already started to walk round. Look, everyone seems to be going. Come on, Joel, I'll race you.

Joel: Oh no you won't!

Narrator: The two boys ran off at top speed, overtaking even the first walkers within a minute or two.

Other boys saw them running, and began to run too. Soon there was quite a group pounding along the pebbly beach. The hot sun and the rough surface soon had them puffing hard and slowed them considerably.

Mark: (*triumphantly, panting hard*) There they are! They're about a hundred yards offshore. We'll just about make it.

Scene 2   The north shore of the Sea of Galilee.

Narrator: Jesus and his disciples climbed out of Peter's boat. At first the hillside seemed deserted, but two panting, sweating, smiling boys greeted them as they paddled to the beach. A trail of others came behind them along the foreshore.

Philip: (*wearily*) I thought we'd come for a bit of peace and quiet.

Matthew: So did I. I hope he sends them all away.

John: Not a hope. Look at his face.

Narrator: Jesus was greeting the boys with a big grin, and welcoming the gathering crowd kindly.

He set off up a hill near the shore, and sat down with his friends around him. A huge number of people followed him and stood about waiting to see what would happen.

Judas: There must be thousands! I've never seen such a crowd except at Passover in Jerusalem!

James: Nor have I. It's unbelievable! Where have they all appeared from? I didn't know Galilee had so many people.

Narrator: The crowd grew bigger, and the people edged closer to Jesus. He began to talk to them. He told them that God cared for them like a loving father. They enjoyed his stories and sometimes he made them laugh.

Several hours went by. Matthew pulled a face at Thomas.

Matthew: I'm tired.

Thomas: Time's getting on too. Hope he sends them home soon.

Narrator: Finally, Jesus stopped teaching the

crowds and turned to Philip.

Jesus: Where can we buy enough food to give to all these people?

Narrator: Philip didn't notice the twinkle in his eye.

Philip: Buy food for this lot! We can't do that! It'd cost a fortune! And anyway, there isn't a shop for miles.

Bartholomew: Tell them to go off to some of the villages and get food for themselves. There's nothing we can do for them here.

Thaddeus: Let 'em go home. It'll be getting dark within an hour or so.

Jesus: (*firmly*) *You* give them something to eat.

Narrator: The disciples just stared at him blankly.

Philip, Bartholomew and Thaddeus together: But Master, we haven't anything . . .

Narrator: Mark and Joel had overheard the whole conversation. They looked at each other. Mark happened to have a snack with him that his mum had given him that morning. He whispered to Joel.

Mark: Shall I offer it to him?

Joel: How's that going to help?

Mark: I dunno, but I'd like him to have it.

Joel: (*shrugs his shoulders*) Then, take it.

Mark: I daren't.

Joel: Go on!

Narrator: Joel shoved Mark forward so that he almost bumped into Andrew. Feeling rather embarrassed, Mark offered Andrew his picnic.

Mark: Here. You can have this if you like.

Andrew: (*smiling*) Thanks very much.

Narrator: Andrew accepted it with some amusement. He showed it to Jesus.

Andrew: It's not a lot, Master!

Narrator: But Jesus took it gladly, as if it was just

what he'd been waiting for.

Jesus: (*to his disciples*) Get everyone to sit down in groups. Not more than fifty or a hundred in each, or we'll never reach people.

Narrator: The whole hillside was soon dotted with sitting groups. Mark and Joel watched carefully.

Joel: He's got your bag of food and he's giving thanks for it.

Mark: Now he's giving some to his friends. Where did they get those baskets from?

Joel: They must have borrowed them.

Mark: Now they're taking it to the groups. Hey, Joel, d'you realise? Every one of those baskets is full of pieces of bread and fish!

Joel: How many rolls did you have?

Mark: Only five, and a couple of fish.

Joel: This is excellent!

Mark: Look! Everyone's getting lots!

Joel: One of his friends is coming to our group. Let's have a taste. See if it's like your mum's baking!

Narrator: The boys reached out as the basket came near, and got two pieces of bread and a fish each.

Mark: Mmmm. Delicious. Didn't know I was so hungry.

Narrator: Joel had such a large mouthful, he couldn't answer for a minute. Then he spluttered, still chewing:

Joel: They're still at it, look! And there's more in the baskets all the time. They must have given some to everyone now.

Mark: They're coming round again! Seconds! Good stuff. I could do with some more.

Narrator: The boys accepted more bread and a fish each, but half-way through Mark gave up.

Mark: I'm bursting!

Joel: Me too. I can't eat this last bit. Let's leave it

for the birds.

Narrator: Excited chatter was breaking out among the crowds.

First man: Do you realise what's happened?

Second man: Yes, Jesus has made food for us all!

First woman: No, he couldn't have done. You can't make bread out of nothing!

First man: But that's just the point, he has.

Second man: Must be an explanation.

First woman: Go on, then. What is it?

Second man: Oh, I don't know. Magic, or something.

First man: Not likely. He's no conjuror. He's a teacher, a healer.

First woman: People can't normally do things like that, so who is he?

Second man: What are you getting at?

First man: Well, I can't explain it any other way. He must be from God!

Narrator: This mention of God was passed on through the crowd.

A youth: Do you mean you think he's a prophet? The Messiah that God promised to send?

First man: Well, what do you think? Who else can he be?

Narrator: The word spread and people got excited.

First voice: He's the Prophet!

Second voice: He's been sent by God.

Third voice: He's come to lead us!

All the crowd: Yes, Yes! He's the King! Long live the King!

Narrator: Mark and Joel looked at each other in amazement.

Mark: At school, the teachers often told us stories about the coming King. Isaiah said he'd govern the world and bring peace.

Joel: But this man's not a king. He's a carpenter! He's lived all his life in Nazareth. His clothes are just like my dad's. He's not grand at all.

Mark: No, yet look what he's done. He can't be that ordinary. Mum says you can't always go by what people look like.

Narrator: Mark turned to take a last look at Jesus.

Mark: Where's he gone?

Joel: Gone? He was here a second ago.

Mark: Well, he's not here now.

Joel: His friends are picking up all the leftovers. Their baskets are just about full of them!

Mark: Come on, Joel. We'd better be off. It'll be dark before we're home otherwise. Race you again!

Walking on water

*The Sea of Galilee is six hundred feet below sea level,
and is surrounded by hills. The water evaporates
rapidly in the hot summer sun. If cooler air from
the Mediterranean meets this vertical air stream, it
causes great turbulence, giving rise to sudden, viol-
ent storms. When the wind drops, the sea calms fairly
rapidly.*

'Isn't it quiet?' remarked Philip.

'Makes a change from that huge crowd!' laughed
Andrew.

Jesus' friends were sitting on the hillside,
watching the people as they set off for home. Thousands of them streamed away along the lake shore
towards Capernaum, chatting excitedly as they
went, about the man who had managed to make all
those fish and all that bread.

The local people were in no hurry. They wandered
down to their small homes beside the sea, shaking
their heads in amazement.

'Never seen him before. Have you?'

'No, never. Who can he be?'

'I dunno. But he's no ordinary man. Did you see
the way he just kept handing out food? It went on
and on and on . . .'

'I reckon the crowds ate more in half an hour than

this village eats in a week!'

'I'm thinking of going over to Capernaum tomorrow to see him again if he's around. Will you come?'

'Sure. Let's go early. We don't want to miss him.'

Meanwhile the disciples had finished clearing up the leftover scraps of food, and Andrew looked around.

'Where did Jesus go?' he asked.

'I don't know. I didn't see him leave,' answered James.

'It'll be getting dark soon,' Peter remarked, looking at the gathering clouds. 'We can't leave it too late before setting off.'

'He's probably gone to pray somewhere,' suggested John.

'Well, let's go and find him. I expect he's forgotten how late it is,' said Thomas.

'No,' replied John firmly. 'When he's praying, we must leave him alone and anyway he doesn't forget things.'

They sat, staring out across the darkening water, hearing the lap of the waves on the shore, the distant voices from the fishermen's houses down below them, and the brush of the wind through the dry grass.

Andrew's mind went back to the afternoon.

'How many do you think there were in that crowd?'

'Three or four thousand, I guess,' said Philip.

'More,' said Matthew. 'I was counting the groups of fifties and hundreds. There must have been five thousand, at least.'

'Most people I went to had two or three pieces of bread and a fish,' James said, 'so that comes to . . .'

'. . . fifteen thousand pieces of bread and five thousand fish,' Matthew helped him.

'Out of five small loaves and two fish! Fantastic! I still can't believe it! Did it really happen, or was it all a dream?'

'Don't be daft,' Andrew laughed. 'Here are all the baskets of leftovers, and they're no dream. Have a bite and see!'

Everyone chuckled. Then Peter got up.

'Come on, everyone, let's get the boat launched. We can't delay any longer. Jesus will probably catch us up somehow.'

'How?' Thomas began, but no one heard him. They were picking up the baskets and setting off down to the shore, glad to be moving at last.

They pushed the boat out into deeper water and climbed in. It was almost dark now, and the air felt chilly. They began to row. To start with the going was smooth and easy, but after several miles the wind got up.

'This is hard work,' said John. 'Wind's against us, I'm afraid.'

'It's all very well for you fishermen,' shouted Bartholomew above the wind. 'You're used to this, but we're not. My hands are getting blisters on this oar.'

'And my arms are about to come out of their sockets,' complained Matthew.

'Just get your backs into it and pull,' Peter told them unsympathetically. 'Here, Bartholomew. Give me that oar for a bit.'

Bartholomew handed over the oar gladly.

The wind blew harder and harder, tossing the little boat up and down on the waves, and splashing water over them. It had been a long day, and they were all very weary. A glum silence settled over them, as the rowers battled on against the wind.

Suddenly, John gave a startled cry. The others felt fear grip their stomachs. Their hair stood on end.

Far out across the waves they could see something white, moving towards them. It was coming closer! It appeared to be a figure. Was it a ghost? They clung to each other in terror. One or two hid their faces in their hands. Others crouched down low in the boat.

Then a voice called out above the wind, 'Don't be afraid! It's only me!'

'It's Jesus!' John exclaimed as he looked up and recognised the figure of Jesus outlined against the night sky.

'Don't be silly, John! We're miles from the shore,' came Thomas's muffled voice from amongst the baskets where he was hiding.

'See for yourself,' suggested John, and they all gradually plucked up courage and looked. Sure enough, Jesus himself was walking across the water towards them!

As he climbed into the boat, they moved closer together to make room for him, but they were still too scared to speak. He looked into their frightened faces.

'You look as if you'd seen a ghost!' he smiled. 'I'm as real as you are!' And he touched them, on the arm, the shoulder, the leg, whatever part he could reach. As they felt his warmth, they knew it was really Jesus. The relief was so enormous that they began to laugh, until Peter saw that they were rocking the boat so violently that they were in danger of filling it with water.

'Look out!' he shouted. 'We'll sink in a minute if we're not careful!'

As they calmed down, James looked ahead.

'I can just make out the lights of Capernaum', he said. 'That was quick!'

'Quick?' said Bartholomew. 'Felt like all night to

me. Ugh, my hands . . .'

'. . . And my arms,' groaned Matthew.

But Andrew, who knew the lake well, agreed with James.

'Why, I'm sure we'd only got half-way, and now we're here! Great! I could do with a meal and a sleep . . .'

'So could I!' chorused the others.

Only John lingered in the boat with Jesus. He looked at him in wonder. It had been another extraordinary day and night. Was there no end to the amazing things this man could do? What power he had! Who could he be?

A blind man sees

In New Testament days, those who couldn't work survived by begging. Many people passed by the Temple during the day, and it was therefore a good place for beggars.

The pool of Siloam is still there today, on the south side of Jerusalem. It marks the city end of the tunnel built by King Hezekiah to bring water into the city in case of siege.

The Pharisees again object to Jesus healing on the Sabbath. These strict religious leaders had created many petty rules and regulations concerning the Sabbath, and according to these, by healing the man Jesus had 'worked' and therefore broken the law.

Just one more dreary day stretched ahead for Reuben the beggar. He was young but he was blind, so he couldn't get about like other people. He sat, all day, every day, near the Temple, where people passed by all the time, and might throw a little money towards him. If they did, he would hastily feel about in the dust, determined to find it before anyone else grabbed it. It was all he had to live on.

'A penny for a poor, blind man!' he called out, and a coin struck his arm.

'Thank you, sir, thank you,' he muttered, not bothering to lift his head.

'Morning, Reuben,' a friendly man greeted him.

'Morning, friend. Why are there so many people about today? What's the excitement?'

'Oh, it's Jesus from Nazareth, this new teacher. He's been at the Temple for a few days, and he always draws a crowd.'

'Ever heard him speak yourself?'

'Yes, a bit. Talks about the Kingdom of God, whatever that is. The Pharisees hate him.'

Just then, a group of young men came along the street, and noticed the blind man.

'Jesus, why is that man blind? Is it his own fault, or have his parents done wrong?' they asked.

'Neither,' Jesus answered. 'It's so that God's power can be shown in his life.'

The disciples looked at one another and shrugged. They didn't understand what Jesus meant.

As they came closer, Jesus stopped in front of Reuben. He spat on the ground, collected the wet dust in the palm of his hand and mixed it with one finger. Then he crouched down and put some of the mud mixture on Reuben's eyes. Reuben was startled at first, but was soon reassured by Jesus's gentle touch. Then Jesus spoke, 'Now go and wash your face in the Pool of Siloam,' he said.

Reuben didn't ask any questions. He didn't hesitate. This man had commanded him to go to the pool so he got up. Slowly, he shuffled and felt his way along the streets, asking the way to the pool of Siloam, which was over half a mile away.

As he went, he felt excited. Why did Jesus put that stuff on his eyes and tell him to go and wash his face? What would happen next?

At last, he arrived at the pool and very carefully felt his way down the steps to the water. The sound of voices told him that other people were there too, perhaps cooling their feet in the water.

Carefully, he knelt at the edge and reached out to feel the water. Cupping his hands, he began to splash his face, and especially his eyes. How cool the water felt. He washed the dirt off, and then – it happened! He could see the water sparkling in the sun! He could see his own hands and count his fingers! He could see the people. He could see the steps, the wall, the sky. HE COULD SEE!

He jumped up in great excitement. He blinked, fearful that if he shut his eyes, he'd be blind when he opened them again. But no. He could still see. 'I can see!' he called out, to the astonishment of some children nearby who had been watching him curiously. 'I've been blind all my life, and now I can see!' he told them. And off he ran.

'I can run,' he thought, grinning broadly, 'and I shan't fall over anything. I must go and tell everyone.'

Soon he arrived at his own street, and burst into his house panting, 'Mother! Father! I can see! Look! Jesus has made me see!'

His parents stared at him, and when they saw his healthy, normal eyes shining with delight, they hugged him joyfully.

'Isn't it wonderful?' he almost shouted. 'But I can't stay. I must go and show everyone else.' And with that he ran out of the house and down the street.

'Who's that?' asked an old woman. 'It looks like Reuben, but it can't be.'

'Do you mean that beggar who's always near the Temple? It does look rather like him.'

'Yes, he is the beggar! I'm sure it's him.'

'No, it isn't. The beggar's blind. I saw him myself this morning in his usual place, asking for money as always. This man can see perfectly well. Look at him!'

Reuben overheard their talk. 'I *am* the beggar,' he smiled. 'I'm Reuben and I can see! Isn't it great?'

'What happened? How can you see? Tell us more!'

'Jesus was passing by, just near the Temple where I usually sit. He stopped, put this wet stuff on my eyes and said: "Go to Siloam and wash your face in the pool." So I did, and as I was washing, suddenly I could see.'

'How wonderful!'

'That's amazing! Where's Jesus now?'

'I don't know.'

A little later, some of the people who'd heard Reuben's story took him to the Pharisees. It was the Sabbath that day. The Pharisees looked at him. 'Well, what happened?' they asked crossly. And again he told the story.

'Jesus put some mud on my eyes, and I washed my face, and now I can see.'

There was a muttering among the Pharisees, the strict religious leaders. 'Well, this Jesus can't be from God. He's disobeyed the law by healing on the Sabbath,' declared one.

'Quite right, quite right,' agreed another.

'And it's not the first time we've had trouble from that man from Nazareth. No respect for the law . . .'

'Come on, you three. How can a bad man do a thing like this?' said Nicodemus.

'Yes, you're the ones who are blind!' said another, siding with Nicodemus. 'Can't you see goodness when it's staring you in the face?'

'But I tell you, it's the Sabbath! It's not allowed!'

They argued heatedly, and then turned on Reuben.

'You say he cured you from blindness, so what do

you think of him?'

'He comes from God,' Reuben declared.

Again the Pharisees murmured crossly.

'Exaggeration, that's what it is,' said one. 'He probably just had a bit of eye trouble, and the water made it better.'

'Yes, that's probably it. After all, it's impossible to cure blindness.'

'Well, I'm not so sure. Let's talk to his parents,' said one Pharisee.

'Here, you!' he said, pointing to a boy. 'Fetch this man's parents, will you?' The boy ran off to do as he was told.

Quite a crowd had gathered by the time the lad came back with Reuben's mother and father. They looked a bit scared at the sight of the Pharisees.

'Is this your son?' demanded a Pharisee.

'Yes, he is,' they answered.

'Was he born blind?'

'Yes, he's been blind all his life.'

'Well, how come he can see now then?'

'We know that he's our son, and that he was blind from birth, but we've no idea how he can see now, and we don't know who did it. Ask him. He's old enough to answer for himself.'

They said this because they were frightened of being forbidden to go to the synagogue if they said they believed in Jesus. So the Pharisees called Reuben back and questioned him again.

'You must give God the praise. This man who cured you is bad,' they told him.

'I don't know whether he's good or bad, but I'm absolutely sure of one thing: before, I was *blind*, and now I can see!'

'What did he do to you? How did he open your eyes?'

'I've told you once, and you wouldn't believe me. Why do you want me to tell you again? Perhaps you want to become his disciples too?' he suggested mockingly.

'You don't know what you're talking about,' they responded angrily. 'You're just an ignorant, uneducated nobody. *You* want to follow Jesus, but we are Moses' followers. We know that God spoke to Moses, but as for this fellow, we don't know where he comes from.'

'How strange!' exclaimed Reuben. 'You don't know where he comes from, and yet he has given me my sight! Everyone knows that God only hears the prayers of those who really love him. If this man were not from God, he wouldn't be able to do miracles like this.'

'You wretched little man! You scum of the earth!' they scoffed. 'Who do you think you are, trying to teach us? Get out of here! Get away from us! Don't you dare go near the synagogue again. You are expelled from this moment.'

The Pharisees glared at him in fury, and Reuben's heart felt as heavy as lead. It was so wonderful to be able to see, but now this . . . He left the group quickly and went off down the street, kicking the stones idly and wondering . . . He found a quiet spot and sat down to think.

Meanwhile, Jesus heard what the Pharisees had done, and went looking for him. As Reuben sat there, staring at the ground, Jesus came up to him. Reuben didn't look up as two feet almost touched his own.

'Hello,' said Jesus kindly.

'Hello,' Reuben murmured, not feeling like talking. But the feet didn't move.

'Do you believe in the Son of Man?' asked the voice

above him.

Reuben shrugged.

'I don't know who he is, so how can I?'

'You've seen him, and he's talking to you now,' Jesus said.

Reuben looked up, and saw Jesus' face. He fell to his knees in front of him, and held his feet.

'Lord, I believe in you!' he cried.

Lazarus – dead or alive

Burial often took place in a natural cave, of which there were many in the area. The wealthy sometimes had a cave specially hewn into rock for the purpose. Owing to the heat, the dead were buried within hours of death, the body being tightly wrapped in strips of white cloth. A body would be seriously decomposed four days after burial.

In the little village of Bethany, two miles over the hill from Jerusalem, lived a family of one brother and two sisters, and they were friends of Jesus. Their names were Lazarus, Mary and Martha. Jesus often came in for a meal and a rest with them.

But that day, Lazarus was very ill, and Mary and Martha were extremely worried. He lay on his mattress and groaned. He was very hot and he ached all over. Flies buzzed around the room, and there was no breeze to lessen the dreadful heat of the midday sun.

'What shall we do?' whispered Mary, choking back tears.

'Let's send for Jesus,' suggested Martha. 'He'll be able to help.'

So they agreed, and a kind friend from along the street offered to go and find him. But Jesus was twenty miles away down by the River Jordan. The sisters waited anxiously, but after three days, there was still no sign of Jesus.

'He's worse today,' sighed Martha.

That night they took it in turn to sit beside him and hold his hand. Then early in the morning, Martha noticed that Lazarus looked very peaceful. She put her hand on his chest but could find no heartbeat.

'Mary!' called Martha, running to find her. 'Come quickly! I think he's . . .'

Mary came running, and felt Lazarus' pulse. Then they both burst into tears.

'Oh, if only Jesus had come in time . . .' wept Martha. 'Why didn't he come?'

'Yes, he could easily have healed him, and he did love him so,' Mary cried.

The neighbours heard them and came to comfort them, but Mary and Martha were heartbroken. Their brother was dead, and Jesus hadn't come. They felt hurt, puzzled, and angry.

Four days went by. The news of Lazarus' death had reached his friends in Jerusalem, and many walked over the hill to Bethany to comfort Mary and Martha. That morning, a young man came panting to the sisters' door.

'I've seen a group coming up the desert road,' he reported excitedly. 'I think it's Jesus and his friends.'

Martha jumped up. 'Show me where they are,' she said, and she ran after him, leaving Mary in the house.

Sure enough, as they came round the side of a house on the edge of the village, a familiar group of men was walking towards them. They looked hot and dusty, tired from their journey. Martha ran to Jesus, and fell at his feet.

'Lord, if only you'd been here, Lazarus wouldn't

have died! And even now, I know that God will do anything you ask him to do.'

Jesus touched her shoulder and spoke kindly, 'Your brother will come back to life,' he said.

'I know that he will come back to life at the end of time,' Martha answered.

'I am the resurrection and the life,' Jesus told her. 'Anyone who trusts in me will live for ever. Do you believe that?'

'Yes, Lord, I believe that you are the Son of God, the One that God said would come into the world.'

Then Martha turned and ran off to tell Mary. She spoke very quietly, 'Jesus is here. He's asking after you,' she whispered. Mary got up at once to go to him, and quite a few others followed her. As soon as Mary saw Jesus, she fell at his feet. 'Lord, if only you'd been here, my brother wouldn't have died,' she sobbed.

Jesus was deeply stirred in his heart, angry at the death that had caused such sorrow, and very sorry for those who were so upset. 'Where have you buried him?' he asked.

'Come and see, Lord,' they replied, and as they led him to the cave, Jesus wept, putting a comforting arm around one shoulder after another. Other people from the village joined the group making for the cave.

When they got there, Jesus said, 'Take the stone away!'

Martha objected, 'But Lord, he died four days ago. There'll be a terrible smell.'

'Didn't I tell you that if you believed, you would see the glory of God?'

No one understood what he meant, but they shrugged and went over to heave the stone away.

Joshua, the son of the village potter, watched with

his mother.

'What are they doing?' asked Joshua. 'Why are they pushing that stone away? Are they going to bring him out again?'

'Shhh! I don't know. Wait and see.'

At that moment Jesus lifted his head and prayed. 'Father, thank you for hearing me. You always do, but I'm saying this for the sake of all these people, so that they may believe that I come from you.'

Then Jesus called loudly, 'Lazarus! Come out!'

The crowd stood waiting, every eye on the cave entrance. Joshua kept very close to his mother. The sun shone brightly and it was difficult to see into the dark opening. Then there was a loud gasp. Someone whispered loudly, 'He's coming out! Lazarus is coming out!'

The stiff, white figure of Lazarus could just be seen in the shadows of the cave entrance. He was completely bound in the white cloths that were used for wrapping dead bodies. Even his head and face were wrapped, and his hands were held to his sides. His feet were so carefully bound that he could only shuffle forward with great difficulty.

No one moved. Everyone was scared stiff. They stared at the slowly moving figure and held their breath.

'Is he dead or alive, Mum?' asked Joshua, very white-faced.

'I – I don't know . . . Alive, I think . . .'

'But he was put there before Dad went to fetch the new donkey four days ago. How come he's still alive?'

'He's not "still alive", Joshua. He was *dead*.'

'But I don't get it. Which is he? Alive or dead?'

'Oh Joshua, I don't know. Just wait a minute. Let's see what happens.'

A few moments later, Jesus spoke calmly, 'Get the cloths off and set him free,' he told the people standing near. After hesitating a moment, one or two moved forward nervously to start undoing the bandages. They undid his head, and the pale but smiling face of Lazarus blinked at them in the sunlight. Mary and Martha rushed forward to hug their brother.

An excited buzz of chatter came from the crowd. Many people were asking, 'Could Jesus be from God?'

Joshua couldn't work it out.

'Mum, did Lazarus just get well again?'

'No, Joshua. He didn't. That kind of thing doesn't happen! Jesus must have done it.'

'Done what? I mean, d'you think Jesus gave Lazarus a new life after he'd been dead for four days?'

'Well, I don't know how else to explain it. After all, we saw him buried, and look, there he is alive, and looking better every minute.'

'Our teacher at school says that when the Messiah comes, he'll do all kinds of miracles. D'you think Jesus could be . . .?'

His mother shook her head.

'I don't know, Joshua, I really don't. What do you think?'

What a party!

Meals were normally eaten at a very low table. Chairs were not used. The participants lay with their heads towards the table, propped up on an elbow. They ate with their fingers.

The ointment used to anoint Jesus' feet was made from spikenard, which grows in India. It was imported into Israel in sealed alabaster jars to preserve the perfume, and was extremely expensive. Spikenard was used for healing and to anoint the dead, so Mary's act was a sign of Jesus' imminent death.

In letting down her hair, Mary was going against convention, for women did not do this in the presence of men. The washing and drying of feet was the task of a slave, so Mary was also demeaning herself greatly in drying Jesus' feet.

It was springtime. Birds were singing. The sun was shining. The air was fresh and clean, bringing the gentle scent of wild flowers into the little house in Bethany. Martha sang as she worked, kneading dough to make bread, cutting up vegetables and pieces of lamb – a special treat – to make a delicious stew for tonight's party.

Mary was happy too, as she dusted the bowls and took out the large jars they would need for the evening meal.

Lazarus was busy rearranging the room and pulling out the table ready for all the guests who were expected.

'It's going to be very crowded,' he said to his sisters.

'Never mind,' said Martha. 'The more the merrier. Just think what it was like when he last came ... and now you're fit and well. We've got so much to celebrate!' Martha was talking about Jesus' last visit to Bethany, when Lazarus had died and everyone was desperately sad. Now he was alive again, and helping to get the party ready.

Joshua came by on his way home from the synagogue, where he and the other boys did their lessons with the rabbi teacher.

'Hi, Joshua,' called Lazarus.

'Hi, Lazarus. You look busy.'

'We are!' he answered. 'We're having a big party tonight to celebrate my being alive again. We've invited Jesus and his friends, and your mother and father; and lots of other friends from the village and from Jerusalem are coming too.'

'Can I come too? And Anna?' asked Joshua.

'If your parents agree,' said Lazarus. 'It might be a bit boring, but you could help pass the food and wine round if you like.'

'Oh, yes please,' said Joshua. He ran off home to find his sister Anna.

'We can go and help at the party tonight!' he told her excitedly. 'I'm sure mum will let us. Jesus will be there, and Lazarus, and lots of people ...'

Evening came at last, and the guests began to arrive.

'Come in, come in,' said Mary, standing by the door and smiling.

A delicious smell of fresh bread, spicy lamb stew and wine, filled the one room of the house, as people went in and greeted each other. There were cheeses, raisins and dates on the table too.

Lazarus called across to Martha, who was stirring the big pot of stew. 'He's coming! Jesus is here!'

'Wonderful! I'll just get the bread out and put the stew on the table.'

Mary was so thrilled to see Jesus. 'Oh Lord, it's so good to see you,' she said, giving Jesus a big hug.

'And you, Mary,' he answered. 'You look well and happy tonight.'

'You've given us good reason,' she said. 'Lazarus is really well.'

Just then, Lazarus himself appeared at the door, and Jesus took him by the shoulders, 'Lazarus, my friend, it's great to see you! How are you?'

'Strong and fit, thank you, Lord. Better than I've felt for months.' He looked at Jesus very gratefully, but a little embarrassed. How could he thank Jesus properly for bringing him back to life when he had been dead? Jesus smiled, and together they entered the house, followed by Peter, Andrew, John, James and many others.

Mary was full of joy. She didn't usually enjoy parties this much, but tonight was different. Her brother, who'd been dead, was alive and well, and her dear Lord Jesus, whom she loved more than anyone in the world, was here for supper. What more could she possibly want? She felt completely happy.

Joshua and Anna arrived with their parents a few minutes later.

'Martha looks very busy. Go and see if you can help her,' their mother said.

When Jesus had thanked God for the food, Martha invited everyone to begin, while she poured the wine. The guests lay, propping themselves up on their elbows around the table. They helped themselves to fresh warm bread. Breaking pieces off with their fingers, they dipped them into the stew and then ate with obvious enjoyment. Martha had added extra spices and the result was delicious.

'You haven't lost your touch, Martha,' said Andrew appreciatively.

'The best ever, Martha,' said Philip with his mouth full.

Lazarus was close to Jesus, and noticed that he too was eating enthusiastically. Joshua and Anna fetched more bread when it was needed, and Joshua tried pouring out some wine, but the jar was heavy and he spilt a bit.

'Never mind,' Martha said kindly. 'Could you bring some more grapes and figs please. That would be a great help.' Joshua was very grateful to her for not being cross.

No one except Anna saw Mary leave quietly, or noticed her coming back with a beautiful stone jar in her hands. Anna watched her and wondered what was in the jar. It was quite big, and she held it with great care as if it were very valuable. The jar was sealed, but she managed to break the seal, and went over to where Jesus was lying. Kneeling by his feet, she bent down, pouring the contents of the jar all over his feet.

'What a funny thing to do,' Anna thought. Then the beautiful perfume of the ointment reached her. She took a deep breath. Mmmm. It was the loveliest smell she'd ever come across. She beckoned to Joshua, who had to clamber over the legs of several guests to get to her.

'Look, Joshua. Mary's poured all that stuff on Jesus' feet. Can you smell it?'

'Of course I can. You mean his head, not his feet, don't you?'

'No, his feet. I saw her do it. Why should she do that?'

'Don't ask me. Sounds a weird idea to me.'

As they watched, Mary put the jar down and bent even lower, undoing her long dark hair and letting it fall over her head and face. As the strong smell of the perfume filled the room, she carefully began to wipe the extra ointment from his feet with her hair.

Anna could hardly believe her eyes. The guests gradually stopped talking as they smelt the ointment, and when they saw what Mary was doing, they stared at her, amazed. Some frowned in disapproval. Others shrugged as if to say, 'She's crazy.'

Jesus turned towards Mary, and his expression was one of deep love and gratitude. He smiled at her warmly, for he understood just how generous a gift it was. The perfume was the most expensive and precious thing she had, and she had given it all to him.

Then Judas spoke out, 'What a dreadful waste!' he said. 'That perfume's worth a fortune. We could have sold it and fed the poor for weeks with the money.'

Judas wasn't really bothered about the poor. He was thinking of himself, because it was his job to look after the money people gave to Jesus, and he would have helped himself to some of it if he'd had the chance.

Mary looked up through her damp hair and caught Jesus' eye. Judas' remarks had hurt her, and she wondered now whether she'd done the wrong thing, but Jesus was reassuring. 'Leave her alone, Judas,' he said. 'She's done a beautiful thing to me. You will always have poor people you can help, but you won't always have me.'

Anna turned to Joshua. 'Joshua,' she whispered, cupping her hands over his ear so that no one else could hear. 'I think Mary did it because she loves Jesus very much.'

Joshua shrugged, 'Funny way of telling someone you love them! I'm going outside for some air. Get away from this smell. Coming?'

'No thanks,' said Anna. 'I'd rather stay here.'

The king is coming!

It was Passover, one of the greatest festivals of the Jewish year. Everyone who could, tried to be in Jerusalem for the celebrations. Bethany is only two miles north of the city, so many travellers passed by the village on their way to Jerusalem.

The prophet Zechariah predicted that the king of the Jews would come into Jerusalem riding on a donkey. A king would usually ride on a horse. To ride a donkey was a sign of humility and of peace. No donkey who had never been ridden before, would normally allow a rider on his back without protest, especially when surrounded by shouting, excited people.

'Hosanna' means 'Save now!' The Jews expected the Messiah to save them from Roman rule and to become their spiritual leader as well.

'Wake up, you two!' called Joshua and Anna's mother. 'How much longer are you going to lie there? The sun's been up for an hour already.'

Joshua and Anna groaned sleepily. They'd had a late night because of the wonderful celebration party at Mary and Martha's house. Everyone had been so happy, because Lazarus was alive again, and Jesus and his friends had come to join the feast.

Mrs Samson put some goat's milk, bread and fruit

ready for Joshua and Anna's breakfast.

'When you've had something to eat, we'll go out and see what's happening,' she said.

'Happening?' said Joshua, jumping up. 'What's happening?'

'The hillside is full of people travelling to Jerusalem for Passover. Lots of our friends are planning to go with Jesus and his disciples. They'll be on their way soon.'

'Can we go?' asked Anna, now wide awake. 'I want to go with Jesus. Please, Mum, will you and Dad come with us?'

'Probably, but first, eat your breakfast.'

They were just finishing when they heard Dad's voice outside.

'Here, what do you think you're doing? That's my new donkey.'

'Jesus needs him,' replied a man's voice.

'Oh well, in that case . . . all right then, but he's not broken in yet. I only bought him the other day, so he's rather wild. The children have named him Frisky.'

'That's very kind of you,' said another man. 'Thank you very much.'

Joshua looked out. He recognised the men. They were two of Jesus' friends who'd been at the party. 'Dad, whatever are they taking Frisky for?'

'I don't know, son, but it's Jesus who wants him, so he'll be all right.'

Soon the whole family went outside.

'Look,' said Anna, pointing. 'What's going on?'

At that moment, they saw a strange sight. Along the village street came a group of Jesus' friends, and in the middle, riding on Frisky, was Jesus!

'He's sitting on a pile of clothes!' said Anna, 'and Frisky's being very quiet. He doesn't even seem to be frightened.'

'Look at his ears,' said Dad. 'He's listening to everything, isn't he?'

Frisky's ears flopped forwards, sideways or backwards all the time, trying to make out the new sounds he was hearing.

'Can we follow them?' said Anna.

'Yes, we'll go with them,' answered Dad, ruffling Anna's dark curls. 'You always want to be in the middle of everything, don't you, Anna?' he smiled.

The little procession began to wind its way round the hill, until the whole city of Jerusalem suddenly came into view across the valley.

'Look, Dad,' said Joshua. 'I can see a crowd of people coming towards us. Why are they coming out of the city when everyone else is going in?'

'Perhaps they're coming to meet Jesus.'

'But they don't know he's here, do they?'

'Someone may have spread the news.'

As they were walking along, more travellers began to join them, and a few of the older people remembered the words of Zechariah the prophet about a king riding a donkey into Jerusalem.

Suddenly someone shouted, 'Long live the King!' Then another joined in: 'God bless the King!'

'Blessed is he who comes in the name of the Lord!'

The crowd became excited.

'Hosanna! Save us!' they shouted, and Joshua and Anna and all the other children joined in, skipping and jumping up and down in their joy. 'Hosanna! Save us! Hosanna to the King!'

People began to cut palm branches off the trees and put them on the road for the donkey and Jesus to walk over. Others took off their cloaks and spread them on the track.

'Get me a branch please, Dad. I can't reach,' said

Anna.

Joshua was already collecting some, and his hand was bleeding where he'd torn a branch down, but he didn't mind.

'Hosanna! Save us!' he shouted loudly, as he laid some more branches in front of Jesus.

The happy procession rounded a steep corner on the way down the Mount of Olives. Joshua grabbed his father by the arm.

'Dad, here comes the crowd we saw before. Look, they're joining in! Frisky won't walk a single step on the road at this rate, he'll have branches and cloaks all the way!'

The noise and the shouting grew louder and louder as the ever-growing crowd made its way down into the valley and began to climb up the other side into the city. The boys and girls were dancing round Jesus, waving palm branches and calling out, 'Hosanna! Hosanna to the King!'

Jesus' friends were a bit puzzled. They didn't really understand what was going on, and Jesus' face was almost sad.

Joshua and Anna were hoarse with shouting, and exhausted from running to and fro with more and more branches. The sun was now high in the sky, and it was very hot.

'Mum, I'm thirsty!' said Anna.

'So am I,' said Josh. 'May we have a drink please?'

'And where do you think I could find a drink from around here? We'd better go home.'

'Oh no, I don't want to go home,' said Joshua. 'I want to go on. Can Dad take me?'

'No, Josh,' Dad answered. 'It's getting too hot and crowded now, and we've had a wonderful morning. Time to be getting back.'

Joshua looked very disappointed, but he didn't

argue because he was so thirsty.

'Mum,' said Anna, as they wearily climbed the Mount of Olives again, picking their way through the branches on the track. 'Is Jesus really a king? He doesn't dress like one.'

'I don't know, dear. There's something very different about him. Think how pleased he was with Mary last night when she poured that expensive perfume on his feet. Think of the way he brought Lazarus to life again when he'd been dead for four days. He's not just an ordinary man, is he?'

'No, certainly not,' agreed Dad, 'I've been at the Temple when he's been teaching sometimes, and he says some amazing things. One day he said, "If anyone's thirsty, let him come to me and drink . . ." '

'I wish he was here now!' said Joshua, feeling thirstier than ever. 'But Dad, if he's a king, what country is he king of? I don't understand. And where's his palace? And shouldn't he have a horse, not our little Frisky, to ride?'

'And wouldn't he be rich?' asked Anna.

Dad shook his head.

'It's strange,' he said, half to himself, mopping his wet forehead with his sleeve. 'Perhaps when we've seen a bit more of him, we'll understand better . . .'

Clean feet

Every Jewish family celebrated Passover with a special meal. This included roast lamb, bitter herbs and unleavened bread, to commemorate the occasion when God 'passed over' the houses where the blood of the lamb had been sprinkled on the door-posts. See Exodus chapter 12.

The bitter herbs signified the bitterness of their years of slavery in Egypt. The unleavened bread showed that the first Passover was prepared and eaten in a hurry, as the people were escaping from Egypt.

It was this meal that Jesus and his disciples were eating together, when Jesus disrobed and did the job of a slave by washing his disciples' feet.

More and more people were crowding into the city of Jerusalem. They came from all over the surrounding area, to celebrate the great feast of Passover. It was the time when the Jewish nation remembered how God had rescued them from being slaves in Egypt hundreds of years before, and had given them their very own country.

All over the city, people were eating the Passover meal of roast lamb, bitter herbs and flat bread, baked without any yeast, as they had done every year since the first Passover.

Jesus and his friends had been lent a big upstairs room for the occasion.

'Mmm, I'm hungry!' said Peter, enjoying the delicious smell of roast lamb.

'So am I,' said Andrew. 'It seems ages since we last had a proper meal together.'

They were all having supper round a long, low table, each one lying propped up on an elbow and reaching for food with the other hand.

It was dark in the room, with only a few flickering oil lamps on the table and around the alcoves. The disciples were nervous. Jerusalem felt more and more dangerous. The religious leaders were very angry with Jesus and wanted to get rid of him. Jesus' friends were scared of what might happen.

Jesus broke the silence, 'I've been longing to share this meal with you before I suffer,' he said, as he looked round at them all.

Only Jesus knew that the next day he would die. His heart was heavy, and he really needed the company of his closest friends. How he loved them! Sometimes, they were confused about what was going on or did not understand what he was talking about, but they had stuck with him through it all.

In the middle of the meal, Philip nudged Thomas, 'What's Jesus doing? He's taken his cloak off and tied a towel round his waist.'

'He's filling the foot basin with water!' exclaimed Thomas. 'Is there a servant coming to wash our feet, do you think?'

It was normally the job of the lowest servant to wash the feet of guests who came to a meal, but of course, no one had done this for Jesus and his friends, as they were using a borrowed room.

'Thomas, he's bringing the bowl over here!' exclaimed Philip. 'It looks as if he's going to do the job himself!'

'But he can't! He's our Master . . .'

'Stretch out your feet, Philip, please. I want to wash them,' said Jesus.

Philip was very embarrassed. He felt his cheeks burning, but Jesus held out his hands, waiting. Reluctantly, Philip took off his sandals, and lifted one foot, then the other. Jesus washed them carefully, and dried them with the towel.

Then Jesus moved on to Thomas, Bartholomew, Matthew, Judas, and all the others. Each one felt awkward and embarrassed, letting Jesus do the servant's job while they lay back like guests.

'You're never going to wash my feet!' Peter objected loudly, drawing his feet up under him, out of Jesus' reach.

'You don't understand now what I'm doing, Peter, but later on, you will,' Jesus answered patiently.

But Peter protested, 'I'll never let you wash my feet!'

'If I don't, you will not really belong to me,' said Jesus.

Peter gulped. Not really belong to Jesus? That was too terrible to think about. 'Then you must wash my hands and my head as well,' he said, getting up to come closer to Jesus.

'I don't need to do that,' Jesus assured him. 'It's only your feet that get dirty as you walk along.'

Peter frowned. He still didn't understand, but he let Jesus wash and dry his feet. When Jesus had finished, he put the bowl aside, took the towel off, put his cloak back on, and sat down alongside his friends again. They all looked at him, waiting for some kind of explanation.

'Do you understand what I've just done?' he asked. They shook their heads.

'You call me "Lord" and "Teacher" and you're right. That's what I am. Yet I've done for you a job that a servant would do. I want you to serve each other in the same way that I've served you.'

The disciples looked at one another, stunned. Wash each other's feet? Why? When?

'But we're not servants,' Thomas whispered to Andrew.

'Nor's he,' replied Andrew.

'No, I know,' Thomas said crossly, 'but he does such odd things. Surely he doesn't want us to do the same?'

'That's what he said,' Andrew answered.

'Peter's feet and yours stink of fish half the time!' said Matthew, joining in.

'Shhh, Matthew,' said John. 'Can't you see? Jesus means we must be willing to do anything for each other, and never think we're too important.'

'Sometimes I find that hard to do,' said Thomas.

'We all do at the moment,' said John, 'but maybe he'll change all that . . .'

On trial

The Garden of Gethsemane was a favourite place of Jesus and his disciples. It lay across the Kidron Valley, not far from the city of Jerusalem, and offered peace and solitude from the turmoil of the city itself.

The Council, or Sanhedrin, was the highest religious authority of the Jews. It was headed by the High Priest. Jesus was brought to this Council on the night before he died.

Jesus and his friends had finished their Passover meal, and Judas sneaked out to tell the authorities where they could find Jesus. The oil lamps flickered in the dark room. Jesus spoke to his disciples about many things that were on his heart.

Finally, he prayed for them. Then they all sang a song, blew out the lamps, and went down the steps into the dark street.

'Where are we going?' Philip asked Andrew.

'Probably to the garden,' Andrew answered.

'You mean the one across the Kidron Valley?'

'Yes, that's where he usually goes to be quiet and safe. It feels a bit ... well, a bit scary in the city tonight, don't you think?' Andrew shivered a little, though it wasn't really cold.

The group followed Jesus out through the city gate, down into the dark valley where the Kidron

Brook gurgled through the trees. Up the other side they went, and in among the old olive trees of the Garden of Gethsemane. One or two birds flew startled out of the trees, and then it was silent except for the gentle rustling of leaves in the night breeze.

Jesus took Peter, James and John further into the garden with him.

'Stay here and keep awake with me,' he begged them. 'I need to have you near.'

Then he went a little way ahead and fell on his face to the ground, crying out to God, and weeping until his whole body shook. He knew that he must soon die on the cross, and it was almost more than he could bear. He went to find his three friends, but they were fast asleep.

'Couldn't you stay awake even for a little while?' he asked sadly. 'Wake up now! They're coming to arrest me.'

They all shook themselves awake, feeling rather ashamed, and got up hastily. They followed Jesus to where the others were waiting.

Thomas was peering through the darkness. 'Look!' he said. 'Soldiers and lanterns! Whatever's happening?'

'They're armed!' said Philip, 'and they're coming this way.'

Jesus' friends were scared stiff.

'Why, that's Judas with them, isn't it? What's *he* doing there?'

As the troop of soldiers and Temple guards appeared through the trees, Jesus stepped forward and spoke to them. 'Who are you looking for?' he asked.

'Jesus of Nazareth,' they answered.

'I am he,' said Jesus calmly, and as he spoke,

all the soldiers staggered backwards and fell to the ground.

'Perhaps he's going to see them off!' said James, hopefully.

But as the soldiers scrambled to their feet, Jesus asked them again: 'Who are you looking for?'

'Jesus of Nazareth,' they replied.

'I told you that I am he. You must let these men go.'

At that, the guards and soldiers stepped forward to arrest Jesus, but Peter couldn't stand it. He drew his sword and lashed out at one of the men, cutting off his right ear.

'Put your sword away, Peter,' Jesus told him. 'I must do what my Father has told me to do.' And he touched the man's ear and healed it.

Then the soldiers grabbed Jesus roughly, tying his hands so that the ropes cut into his wrists. They began to push and shove him down through the garden ahead of them.

The disciples were so terrified that they ran away through the trees, all except Peter and John.

'We must take care, Peter,' said John quietly. 'We mustn't be seen, but we've got to know where they take him.'

'It looks as if they're heading for the High Priest's house. We can follow them up the steps at a safe distance,' said Peter. Then he added, 'Oh John, whatever's going to happen now?'

John shook his head but said nothing.

By the light of the flaming torches carried by the soldiers, Peter and John saw Jesus being taken into the courtyard of the High Priest's house.

'Everyone will be asleep by now, won't they?' said Peter. 'What's the point of bringing him here at night?'

'Perhaps they've called all the Council members specially – woken them up, even. Quick, we'll lose sight of him if we don't hurry.'

They ran up the remaining steps, just as Jesus was taken through the courtyard into the High Priest's Council room. John knew some of the servants who worked there, so they let him into the courtyard.

'May I bring my friend too?' he asked.

'Yes, sure,' answered the girl by the door.

She stared at Peter in the semi-darkness.

'You're one of his friends, aren't you?' she said, jerking her thumb towards the room where Jesus had been taken.

'No, I am not,' Peter lied.

There was a fire in the courtyard, and some of the soldiers gathered round it, rubbing their hands to keep warm. John kept away, but Peter joined the group by the fire.

'You're one of that man's disciples, aren't you?' scoffed a soldier.

'No, I'm nothing to do with him,' Peter lied again, waving his arms about and feeling extremely uncomfortable.

'Oh yes, you are!' declared another man, pointing his finger at Peter's face. 'I saw you in the garden with him!'

'Oh no, you didn't! I don't know the man!' and Peter swore angrily.

Just at that moment, across the city came the sound of an early cock crowing. Peter's mind flashed back to supper-time. He'd promised Jesus that he'd never deny him, even if he had to die with him, and Jesus had answered, 'I tell you, Peter, before the cock crows, you'll say three times that you don't know me.'

He turned from the fire, pulling his cloak around him, and hurried out into the narrow street. Leaning against the wall, he sobbed as if his heart would break.

'How could I do that to you, Lord? How could I say that? You mean the world to me, and I've denied you. How can you ever forgive me? And how can I ever forgive myself? I'm a rotten coward, and I thought I was so brave. Oh Lord, I'm sorry, I'm sorry.'

Could Peter ever face Jesus again?

The cross

The High Priest was the leader of the Jewish religious rulers.

Israel was occupied by the Romans. Caesar, the Emperor, appointed a governor to rule the country, and Pontius Pilate held this position. Pilate was very impressed with Jesus, and convinced of his innocence. He sought for a way to set him free, but the threat of Caesar's disapproval and his own possible removal from office, proved too great.

Flogging was an extremely severe punishment, from which some died. The victim's arms were stretched round a pillar, to expose the back. He was given thirty-nine lashes with a whip to which pieces of metal or bone were attached at frequent intervals. The effect of this was to tear the flesh to the bone, leaving the victim's back completely raw.

Crucifixion was a Roman punishment which Jews were not permitted to use, so Roman soldiers crucified Jesus. Death sometimes took two days or longer, but after six hours, Jesus gave up his life and died. He had finished the work he came to do.

It was very early morning. Jesus had been arrested, and was on trial in the house of Caiaphas, the High Priest, the leader of the Jewish religious rulers. John was the only one of Jesus' friends who was close by. He was watching and waiting to see what would happen. The High Priest questioned Jesus for a long time, and people accused him of various crimes. The Council were trying to find some reason to put Jesus to death, but his accusers couldn't agree with each other.

After a while, the soldiers brought Jesus out and took him to the governor's palace, where they banged on the door. There was a pause, then Pilate the governor appeared, angry at being disturbed so early in the morning.

'What do you accuse this man of doing?' he demanded.

'If he wasn't guilty, we wouldn't have brought him here,' they replied.

But Pilate knew that they were trying to get Jesus condemned to death, and after he had questioned him, he was more certain than ever that Jesus was innocent. He decided to do his best to set him free.

'I find nothing wrong with this man, but you have a custom that I always set a prisoner free at Passover. Shall I release the King of the Jews for you?'

This made the Jewish leaders furious. How dare Pilate call Jesus 'the King of the Jews'? He was just a nobody from Galilee, who'd made a thorough nuisance of himself. They yelled, 'No, we want Barabbas set free! Free Barabbas!'

(Barabbas was in prison for causing riots and for murder.)

By now, quite a crowd had gathered. They began to join the shouting. 'We want Barabbas! We want Barabbas!'

John heard the shouts, and his heart sank. Peter too, was on the edge of the crowd.

Pilate went inside the palace with Jesus and the soldiers, and the crowd waited outside.

'It's unfair, that's what I think,' said an old man.

'Disgraceful! He never did anyone any harm,' agreed another.

'Kill him! Kill him! He's a trouble-maker,' said others, urged on by the Jewish leaders.

'Get rid of him! A king indeed! Whatever next? The Emperor Caesar's the only king around here.'

'But he's been teaching in the Temple for weeks. He talked about God loving everyone, and how we need to be forgiven,' said a younger woman.

'I saw him heal people too. He was always kind,' added another.

The Jewish leaders were stirring up the crowd and the shouts against Jesus grew louder and louder.

'Crucify him! Crucify him!'

John and Peter were horrified. Kill their Lord! Crucify him! It was too terrible to think about.

Then Pilate came out, and ordered Jesus to be brought in front of the people. There was a loud gasp in the crowd, and John hid his face in his hands. For blood was trickling down Jesus' face.

'They've rammed a crown of thorns on his head,' said someone.

'He can hardly walk,' said another. 'I bet they've flogged him.' (Flogging was a dreadfully cruel punishment which often killed a man.)

John could hardly bear to look at Jesus, who stood very still, very calm, but bowed in pain. Was this really happening? It seemed like a terrible nightmare.

'Here he is!' said Pilate, pointing to Jesus. 'I cannot find that he's done anything wrong.'

'Crucify him! Crucify him!' shouted the crowd.

'*You* crucify him,' said Pilate. 'I can find nothing he's done wrong.'

80

'He claims to be the Son of God, and in our law, the punishment for that is death,' shouted the Jewish leaders.

Pilate was scared when he heard this, and took Jesus inside the palace again to question him further. He came out even more sure that Jesus was not guilty, but the people yelled loudly, 'Kill him! Kill him! If you set him free, you're an enemy of Caesar!'

In the end, Pilate gave in and handed Jesus over to them to be crucified.

John knew now that the end had come. There was no hope for Jesus. He found Jesus' mother, Mary, weeping, and put an arm round her as they followed the grim procession up the hill.

Three men were crucified that day, two robbers and Jesus. As Jesus' cross was lifted up and put in the ground, Mary and John, and a few other women, gathered at his feet. Jesus saw Mary there, and spoke to her, 'John is your son now,' he said to her. Then he said to John, 'Take her as your mother.'

From that day onwards, John took Mary home with him and cared for her.

Meanwhile, Pilate gave orders for a board to be nailed above Jesus' head with the title, 'Jesus of Nazareth, the King of the Jews'.

'Don't say that,' the Jewish leaders objected. 'Say: "This man *said* he was king of the Jews." ' But Pilate refused to change it.

'What I've written, I've written,' he said firmly, and that was the end of the matter.

'It's getting dark!' the people said to one another. 'It's like night in the day!'

'The sun's turning black!'

'I'm scared! Let's get home quickly!'

Fear swept through the crowds, and many ran

stumbling home along the eerily dark streets.

'What's happening?' they asked each other, but no one understood. They just felt a terrible sense of evil everywhere.

Some didn't go home, but hung around to see how it would all end. A cold wind swept across the hillside. Mary shivered. John took off his cloak and wrapped it round her. A strange silence came over everyone.

It was dark for three hours, but as it gradually began to get light again, Jesus broke the silence, crying out in a loud, triumphant voice, 'It is completed!' Then he bowed his head and died.

John spoke to Mary in a low voice, 'I think he means that he's finished the work he came to do.'

Mary nodded through her tears but couldn't speak.

'Come on,' said John gently, 'I'll take you home.' And he led her away down the hill.

Alive again!

Near Golgotha, 'the place of a skull,' where Jesus was crucified, was a garden. The garden may well have belonged to Joseph of Arimathea, one of Jesus' secret disciples. Nicodemus was another secret disciple. He had once visited Jesus by night so that he would not be seen (see John chapter 3). The two men took the body of Jesus down from the cross.

A new tomb had been hewn in the rock in the garden, ready for Joseph's own use when he died. He gave his tomb to Jesus.

Joseph and Nicodemus were both wealthy, so they embalmed Jesus' body with spices, according to the custom of the rich. The spices were mixed with plaster, which would make the mixture set completely rigid when it dried. Then they wrapped layers of white cloth round the body before placing it in the cave tomb. Finally, they heaved a very large, circular stone across the entrance. This stone would be extremely difficult to move.

Soon after Jesus had died on the cross, two of his friends came and carefully took his body down. They wrapped it in clean cloths, and put it in a small cave in a nearby garden. Then they heaved a great stone across the entrance, and went away. Some of the women who knew Jesus best were watching, so they knew where he was buried.

The next day was the Sabbath day of rest, so no one could do anything, but very early on Sunday morning, Mary Magdalene woke up. She sat up and looked out. It was still dark. 'I must get to the cave,' she thought, leaping up and pulling on her cloak and sandals.

She walked quickly along the dark streets to the garden, but when she arrived and looked towards the cave, she gave a shout of horror and despair. The great stone had been rolled away from the entrance, and she could see the dark opening in the early morning light.

Mary turned and ran back as fast as she could to tell Peter and John. Banging on the door of the house where they were staying, she burst in. 'They've taken the Lord out of the cave, and I don't know where they've put him!' she cried.

Peter and John jumped up at once and ran towards the garden, while Mary followed. John ran faster than Peter and arrived panting at the cave. He stared in and could just see some cloths lying on the floor, but he didn't go in. Peter came puffing along behind, and went straight into the cave.

'Look, John, these are the cloths they used for wrapping his body, aren't they?'

'They must be,' said John, 'and they're in the exact shape of his body too.'

'Yes,' said Peter. 'Here's the wide part of his shoulders, and look, this separate cloth was round his head. It's in just the position where he must have been laid.'

'Yet there's no body!' said John. 'Where is it? How could it get out from the cloths like that?'

'. . . And leave them undisturbed?' said Peter.

There was a glimmer of hope in John's eyes: 'Could he be . . .?'

'Alive? Impossible! But I don't see how ... Oh come on, John, let's get back and tell the others.'

The two men forgot all about Mary Magdalene, and left her alone in the garden, crying. When they'd gone, she quietly walked to the cave entrance and looked in. Then she gasped, for there in the cave sat two men dressed all in white, one where Jesus' head had been, and one by his feet.

'Why are you crying?' they asked her gently.

'Because they've taken my Lord away, and I don't know where they've put him,' Mary sobbed.

As she cried, she became aware of someone behind her. She turned, assuming that he was the gardener coming to work.

The man spoke to her. 'Why are you crying? Who are you looking for?' he asked.

'Oh, sir, if you've taken him away, please tell me where you've put him, so that I can go and find him,' she begged.

The man spoke again, using her name. 'Mary!'

At once Mary recognised the voice of Jesus. She looked up through her tears. 'My Lord!' she exclaimed joyfully, falling to her knees in front of him. She would have held his feet, but Jesus stopped her.

'Don't touch me now, but go and tell my friends that I'm going back to be with my Father.'

Mary looked up. Yes, it was definitely Jesus! She was so excited that she wanted to shout, 'He's alive! Jesus is alive!' She wanted to spread the news to the whole world! She jumped to her feet and ran to the others, who were all gathered round Peter and John, puzzling over the strange news they had brought.

Mary burst into the room. 'I've seen Jesus!' she told them. 'He's alive! He spoke my name, and I recognised his voice. He told me to come and tell you . . .'

They looked at her doubtfully.

'It's true! I promise you! I thought he was the gardener, and asked him if he'd taken the body away, then he said, "Mary!" and I knew it was him.'

Peter and John looked at each other. It was too good to be true. They hardly dared believe it, yet what about those cloths in the cave? It all seemed to make sense, and yet *they* had not seen Jesus. They only had Mary's word for it.

That evening, the disciples were all together except Thomas. They talked quietly, scared of being discovered and arrested. For now that Jesus was dead, they feared it would be their turn next.

'Let's bolt the door!' Philip suggested, and when he'd done it they felt a little safer.

Suddenly, the room became lighter, and there among them stood Jesus, smiling. They drew back from him in fear and shock. Some hid their faces in their hands. No one said a word.

Then Jesus spoke. 'Peace be with you!' he said.

They knew his voice at once. He spoke quietly and gently, as if to reassure them. Then he showed them the wounds in his side and hands and feet. Gradually, they began to realise that it really was Jesus, and that he really had come back to life.

Wonderful joy filled their hearts. Some touched his feet and some his hands. Others simply gazed at him in amazement. How could he be alive? They had seen him killed! Yet they couldn't deny what they were seeing with their eyes. Jesus was alive again! It was the best news of all time!

Breakfast on the beach

The first part of the story takes place in the upper room in Jerusalem where Jesus ate the Last Supper with his disciples. Since his death, his friends had spent most of their time there, behind locked doors, afraid of imminent arrest.

The second part takes place in Galilee, a province of Israel that is situated seventy miles north of Jerusalem. This is where Peter and Andrew, James and John lived and worked as fishermen until Jesus called them to follow him. The story is presented as a dramatic reading.

Scene 1 An upstairs room in Jerusalem. Late evening.

Narrator: Some of Jesus' friends had gathered in an upstairs room. They had locked the door and were in hiding. The room was lit by a few flickering oil lamps. It was late and the friends were talking quietly but excitedly. Jesus had just been with them. He had shown them his wounds and said, 'Peace be with you.' The joy of his presence lingered with them in the room. Suddenly there was an urgent knocking at the door. They started up, afraid of being arrested.

Thomas: (*in a loud whisper*) Let me in, quick!

Philip: Oh, Thomas, thank goodness it's only you!

We thought it was soldiers . . .

Peter: Thomas, we've seen the Lord!

Andrew: He was here a moment ago! You've just missed him!

John: He spoke to us and said, 'Peace be with you,' and he showed us his wounds.

Bartholomew: He never opened the door! He just came and stood among us.

Philip: I touched his feet!

James: And I touched his hand!

Andrew: It was light in here while he was with us, but now it's gone dark again.

Narrator: Thomas looked from one to another in astonishment and disbelief. He shook his head, feeling bewildered and angry.

Thomas: Absurd! Impossible! I'll never believe it unless I can put my finger into the wounds in his hands and put my hand in his side!

Narrator: A week later, Jesus' friends were again in the room with the door bolted, and this time Thomas was with them. Suddenly, Jesus appeared among them.

Jesus: Peace be with you! (*He turns to Thomas*). Put your finger in my hands and put your hand in my side. Stop doubting and believe the truth. I really am alive!

Narrator: Thomas was overcome and fell at Jesus' feet.

Thomas: My Lord and my God!

Jesus: Thomas, you believe because you've actually seen me with your own eyes. How happy are those who believe that I'm alive, even though they've never seen me!

Scene 2   Galilee.

Narrator: A little while after Jesus appeared to his friends in Jerusalem, they decided to leave the city and go back north to Galilee. It was a three or four day walk in burning heat from Jerusalem to Galilee over hilly countryside. Towards Galilee the land drops steeply down, for the Sea of Galilee lies six hundred feet below sea level. The disciples chatted as they picked their way along the stony shore to reach their home town, Capernaum.

Andrew: I suppose we might as well take up fishing again, Peter. Don't know what else to do.

Peter: I can't believe it's all over. I mean, these last three years have been so exciting, and now we know Jesus is alive again . . .

James: Don't you think we'll be doing something else with him?

Thomas: How can we? He's not *with* us any more.

Matthew: No, that's what I don't understand.

Narrator: John had been listening and thinking. Now he spoke thoughtfully.

John: Do you remember what he said at supper the night he was arrested? He talked about a Counsellor he was going to send. Someone who would always be with us and would help us just as he has done. He said we'd be better off in the future than if he himself was still with us. Remember?

Narrator: The others shook their heads. They had not understood what Jesus meant. How could it be better *without* him than *with* him?

Narrator: When they saw Capernaum ahead, they cheered up a bit. It began to feel like home. They sat down on the pebbly beach by the Sea of Galilee for a rest. After a while, Peter got to his feet.

Peter: I'm going fishing.

Thomas: I'll come with you.

James, John and three others: So will I!

Narrator: They climbed into Peter's boat, while he checked the nets. It was a long time since he'd last been fishing, and the rats might have gnawed holes in them.

Finally, everything was ready and they set sail in a gentle breeze. The sun was going down, turning the far hills dusky red, and lighting up the ripples on the water. It felt great to be at sea again!

They sailed into deeper water, let down the nets in the gathering darkness, and waited.

James: It doesn't feel as though there are fish in the nets. Shall we try somewhere else?

Peter: Good idea!

Narrator: They hauled the nets in, moved some distance and threw them in again.

An hour went by. Then another.

Peter: (*fed up*) Still nothing. This used to be a good area. I remember some excellent catches here.

John: So do I. Let's try once more.

Narrator: But it was no use. All night long they kept casting their nets but they didn't catch a single fish.

Peter: I've had enough! What a night! After all this time, we spend a whole night fishing and catch nothing! It's enough to put you off for ever!

Nathanael: Must have lost the knack!

Narrator: No one laughed at his joke.

Peter: (*crossly*) Let's make for the shore.

Narrator: Wearily, they pulled in the empty nets, and began to sail back towards Capernaum. Everyone sat in glum silence in the darkness. Only Peter, James and John were kept busy with the boat.

Day broke as they approached the shore. A man, standing on the beach, called to them.

The man: Have you caught anything?

All: No!

The man: Cast your nets on the right of the boat and you'll catch some.

Narrator: Peter was about to tell him that they'd tried all night, but James and John started heaving the wet nets into the water straight away. No sooner were the nets under water than a great stirring began all around the boat.

Thomas: Look! There's fish everywhere! They seem to be almost jumping into the nets!

John: You're right, Thomas, they are. Hang on to the nets or we'll lose them!

James: We'll never be able to get this load aboard. We'd break the nets!

Peter: We'll have to pull them behind the boat. What a catch! And at dawn too!

Narrator: John stared again at the man on the beach. He looked somehow familiar. Could it be Jesus? Who else could give them such a huge catch of fish?

John: It's the Lord!

Narrator: Peter raised his head at once, and looked hard at the figure standing there. John was right! Of course it was the Lord! Without stopping to think, he pulled his robe round him, jumped into the knee-deep water, and waded to the shore as fast as he could.

The others brought the boat in, dragging the net full of fish behind them. As they landed, they noticed a fire on the pebbles, and a delicious smell of cooking fish. There was fresh bread too, and it made them feel really hungry.

Jesus: Bring some of the fish you've just caught.

Narrator: Peter climbed into the boat and pulled the net up onto the beach. He counted the fish as he took them out.

Peter: A hundred ... a hundred and forty ... a hundred and fifty three! A record! I can't ever remember catching so many before! What's more, the net hasn't torn in spite of the extra weight!

Narrator: He brought some fish to Jesus.

Peter: Here you are, Lord. How many more shall I bring?

James: As many as you like, Peter! We're all ravenous!

Narrator: They stood about, not quite sure what to do, while Jesus cooked the fish.

Jesus: Come and have some food.

Narrator: But no one moved, so Jesus picked up some fish and bread and gave it to them.

They ate their breakfast without saying much. They gazed across the water and watched the sunrise, as they enjoyed the hot fish and crunchy bread.

After a while, Jesus beckoned to Peter, and the two of them went off for a walk along the shore. When they'd gone, the others looked at one another.

James: Am I dreaming?

John: No. It's the Lord all right.

James: But he cooked our breakfast! He died two weeks ago ...

John: But we've seen him twice in Jerusalem! Surely you haven't forgotten!

James: No, no, of course I haven't, but this time he actually made a fire, cooked food, and gave it to us ...

John: Well, it just goes to show that he really is alive!

Other resource books for junior children

Line up for Assembly
Joanna Pitkin
Thirty-seven outlines for class assemblies for 7–11s. Each outline provides guidance on preparation with the class, the actual presentation, which is given in full, and a variety of suggestions for follow up activities.

The material is Bible based and the outlines suggest a variety of activities such as singing, drama and painting which involve the whole class.

An introductory section on the nature and characteristics of assembly contains important observations on handling class assemblies.

Maximus Mouse
Brian Ogden
Short stories to enliven junior assemblies or church groups.

Maximus lives in a church vestry and sees himself as the church cleaner. He collects stray paper hankies which he uses to make duvets, and loose pages from hymn books which make good hymnburgers.

He also listens to the vicar's sermons on the Lord's Prayer but does not always get the message quite right.

Each story ends with a brief prayer which summarises the main teaching point.

Maximus Rides Again
Brian Ogden
In response to the popularity of the first book, Brian Ogden has produced more stories about Maximus Mouse and his friends.

Themes of stories include bullying, jealousy and rule-breaking, all dealt with in humorous situations.

These stories have a wide age appeal.